THE NEXT STEP

By J.T.C.

Chick Publications
Chino, California

My deepest appreciation to...
Pastor James L. Franklin
for his help in preparing this book.

INTERNATIONAL DISTRIBUTORS

Christ The Way Publications, Inc.
P.O. Box 43120, Eastwood Square
Kitchener, Ont. N5H 6S9, Canada

B. McCall Barbour
28 George IV Bridge
Edinburgh, Scotland/UK EH1 1ES
Tel: 031-225 4816

New Zealand Evangelistic Society
P.O. Box 50096
Porirua, Wellington, New Zealand

Evangelistic Literature Enterprise
P.O. Box 5010
Brendale, Q'ld., Australia 4500
Tel: (07) 3205-7100

Gospel Publishers
P.O. Box 1
Westhoven 2142, South Africa
Tel: (11) 673-3157
Fax: (11) 673-2644

Sword Distributors
P.O. Box 3459
Parklands 2121, South Africa
Tel/Fax: (11) 486-3361

Chick-Traktate-Versand
Postfach 3009
D-42916 Wermelskirchen
West Germany
Tel. 02174/63815
Fax: 02174/2799

Published by Chick Publications
P.O. Box 662, Chino, CA 91708-0662 USA
Tel: (909) 987-0771 • Fax: (909) 941-8128
http://chick.com

By E-Mail:
   Compuserve: 102132,175
   Internet: 102132.175@compuserve.com

Printed in the United States of America

TABLE OF CONTENTS

WHEN YOU RECEIVED THE LORD JESUS CHRIST AS YOUR OWN PERSONAL SAVIOR, YOU MADE THE MOST IMPORTANT DECISION OF YOUR LIFE.

TO HELP YOU BE MORE EFFECTIVE IN YOUR CHRISTIAN WALK, THIS LITTLE BOOK SHOULD BE MOST HELPFUL.

CHAPTER 1

THE BIRTH OF THE BIBLE

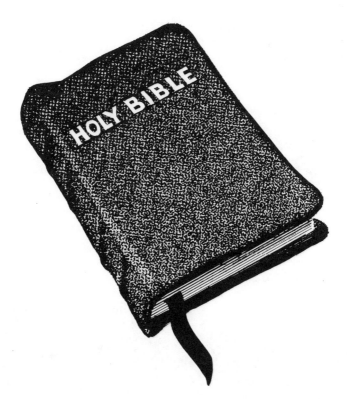

FOR THE PROPHECY CAME NOT IN OLD
TIME BY THE WILL OF MAN: BUT HOLY
MEN OF GOD SPAKE AS THEY WERE
MOVED BY THE HOLY GHOST. 2 Peter 1:21

IN THE FIRST CENTURY OF THE CHURCH, THE HOLY SPIRIT DIRECTED GOD'S CHOSEN APOSTLES TO WRITE THE NEW TESTAMENT SCRIPTURES.

BECAUSE OF THE EARLY CHURCH'S CLOSENESS TO GOD IN PURITY AND UNITY, THEY HAD THE GIFT TO DETECT SATAN'S EARLY FORGERIES AND CAST THEM ASIDE.

ANANIAS AND SAPPHIRA WERE DESTROYED BY GOD BECAUSE THEY THREATENED TO DESTROY THE UNITY OF THE CHURCH THROUGH LYING.   Acts 5:1-11

IN ITS PURITY, THE EARLY CHURCH RECOGNIZED THOSE BOOKS THAT WERE GENUINELY INSPIRED BY GOD.

AS YEARS PASSED, THE PURITY AND UNITY BECAME DILUTED . . . AND NO SUCH AGREEMENT WAS POSSIBLE.

THEREFORE, THE HOLY SPIRIT ANTICIPATED THIS AND COMPLETED THE NEW TESTAMENT BEFORE THIS UNITY WAS BROKEN . . .

SATAN TRIED DESPERATELY TO DESTROY THE EARLY CHURCH AND THE SCRIPTURES.

ROME'S FINAL EFFORT TO BLOT OUT ALL CHRISTIAN SCRIPTURES WAS MADE DURING DIOCLETIAN'S PERSECUTION IN 295-305 A.D.

PAPA MADE ME PROMISE THAT IF THEY TOOK HIM AWAY --- I WAS TO GIVE THIS TO MARCELLUS.

WHAT IS IT?

IT'S A LETTER FROM THE APOSTLE PAUL. HE SAID WE MUSTN'T LOSE IT --- IT'S VERY IMPORTANT.

PRECIOUS LETTERS TO THE CHURCHES WERE COPIED AND KEPT IN SAFE PLACES... UNTIL THE YEAR 313 A.D.

AT THIS TIME, EMPEROR CONSTANTINE ISSUED HIS *EDICT OF TOLERATION IN ORDER TO KNOW HOW MANY CHRISTIANS WERE UNDER HIS AUTHORITY.

THE TERRIBLE TIME OF PERSECUTION FOR THE CHRISTIAN CHURCH ALMOST CAME TO ITS END.

READ CRUSADER STORY #11, "SABOTAGE?" PUBLISHED BY CHICK PUBLICATIONS.

BY THIS TIME ALL OF THE <u>TRUE</u> SCRIPTURES WERE IN THE HANDS OF THE <u>TRUE</u> BELIEVERS.

ALL OF THE EARLY CHURCHES CONSIDERED THE OLD TESTAMENT TO BE THE WORD OF GOD, BECAUSE THE LORD JESUS TAUGHT IT IN THE SYNAGOGUES AND REFERRED TO IT AS SCRIPTURE.

HUNDREDS OF PHONEY BOOKS SHOWED UP AS MANUSCRIPTS. EACH ONE OF THEM CONTRADICTED THE TRUE WORD OF GOD.

THE EARLY CHRISTIANS EXAMINED ALL OF THE BOOKS AND PUT THEM INTO THREE CATEGORIES.

I THOSE UNIVERSALLY ACCEPTED.

II THIS GROUP WAS CALLED "SPURIOUS" BOOKS, SOME OF WHICH WERE THE "ACTS OF PAUL," "SHEPHERD OF HERMIAS," "APOCALYPSE OF PETER," "EPISTLE OF BARNABAS," AND "DIDACHE."

III THIS GROUP WAS LABELED "THE FORGERIES." SOME OF THOSE IN THIS GROUP WERE "GOSPEL OF PETER," "GOSPEL OF THOMAS," "GOSPEL OF MATHIAS," "ACTS OF ANDREW," AND "ACTS OF JOHN."

THE FOLLOWING TESTS WERE MADE TO SEE IF EACH BOOK QUALIFIED TO BE INCLUDED IN THE NEW TESTAMENT.

A. WAS THE BOOK WRITTEN BY AN APOSTLE OR A DISCIPLE OF CHRIST?

C. WAS THE BOOK RECEIVED UNIVERSALLY THROUGHOUT THE TRUE CHURCH?

B. WERE THE CONTENTS OF THE BOOK OF UNQUESTIONABLY HIGH SPIRITUAL CHARACTER?

D. THE ONLY BOOKS ALLOWED WERE THOSE WHICH GAVE ADEQUATE EVIDENCE OF HAVING BEEN DIVINELY INSPIRED.

DURING THAT TIME THE CHURCH LEADERS, WHO LIVED AFTER THE APOSTLES, COULD ONLY AUTHENTICATE WHAT THE EARLY CHURCH "IN THE SPIRIT" ALREADY KNEW WAS GENUINE.

THE AUTHORITY OF SCRIPTURE IS BY --

FIRST . . . . THE HOLY SPIRIT

SECOND . . . . THE TRUE BODY UNIFIED IN THE SPIRIT (TRUE BELIEVERS) HAD THE SPIRIT OF DISCERNMENT.

THIRD . . . . CROSS REFERENCES IN SCRIPTURE MADE BY OTHER WRITERS. FOR EXAMPLE PETER, IN II PETER 3:15-16, SPOKE OF PAUL'S WRITINGS AS SCRIPTURE.

THAT'S HOW WE GOT THE 27 BOOKS OF OUR NEW TESTAMENT.

FOR ALMOST 1500 YEARS SATAN HAS ATTACKED THE SCRIPTURES

IN THESE CLOSING HOURS HE IS EVEN MORE DESPERATE!

HE KNOWS HIS TIME IS SHORT.

NOTE: FOR A BROADER STUDY ON THE BATTLE FOR THE BIBLE, READ CRUSADER STORY #11, "SABOTAGE?" PUBLISHED BY CHICK **PUBLICATIONS.**

CHAPTER 2

DON'T READ THAT BOOK

THIS BOOK OF THE LAW SHALL NOT DE-
PART OUT OF THY MOUTH; BUT THOU
SHALT MEDITATE THEREIN DAY AND
NIGHT, THAT THOU MAYEST OBSERVE TO
DO ACCORDING TO ALL THAT IS WRITTEN
THEREIN: FOR THEN THOU SHALT MAKE
THY WAY PROSPEROUS AND THEN THOU
SHALT HAVE GOOD SUCCESS.   Joshua 1:8

THIS IS THE MOST CONTROVERSIAL, THE MOST HATED AND THE MOST LOVED BOOK EVER PRINTED — IT HAS CAUSED THE DEATH OF UNTOLD NUMBERS AND HAS GIVEN ETERNAL LIFE TO MILLIONS.

THROUGH ITS HISTORY, SATAN HAS LAUNCHED EVERY TYPE OF ATTACK IMAGINABLE AGAINST THOSE WHO LOVE THIS BOOK.

HERE WE ARE IN THE 20th CENTURY AND SATAN IS USING ANOTHER CLEVER TECHNIQUE TO KEEP CHRISTIANS FROM READING IT.

THE ATTACK COMES THROUGH FILMS AND TELEVISION. IF POSSIBLE THE VILLAIN IN THE STORY IS A BIBLE QUOTING NUT, WHO IS USUALLY WORSE THAN FRANKENSTEIN — IN FACT, CHRISTIANS ARE WARNED BY OTHER CHRISTIANS AND THE UNSAVED, NOT TO READ THE BIBLE — THEY COULD GO NUTTY!

(TOUCHÉ, SATAN SCORES AGAIN!)

IN SOME COUNTRIES CHRISTIANS ARE IN DUNGEONS BECAUSE THEY LOVED THE BIBLE. THEY FIND THEIR ONLY COMFORT COMES FROM REPEATING SCRIPTURES THEY HAD MEMORIZED BEFORE IMPRISONMENT.

How would you make out in the same predicament?... you may soon face the same situation.

OUR GREATEST COMPANION IN OUR HOMES IS PROBABLY SATAN'S GREATEST WEAPON—

THE BOOB TUBE—

IT'S BEEN SAID THAT THE AVERAGE VIEWING TIME IS 3½ HOURS DAILY.

LET'S STOP *PLAYING* GAMES!

DOESN'T HE REALIZE WHAT I'M GIVING UP?

GUESS WHAT?—YOU'RE GOING TO DROP ONE OF THOSE STUPID 1 HOUR TV SHOWS—EVERY DAY—AND WE'RE GOING TO GET INTO THE WORD OF GOD!

There have been great Bible study courses put out by many good churches and organizations — because of laziness or indifference or other legitimate reasons these courses collect dust in someone's desk drawer.

Your assignment is in this book —

so keep it where you can see it . . . (incidentally, this book will not self-destruct.)

I HAVE A FRIEND WHO ACTUALLY GLOWS WITH THE LOVE OF JESUS. EVERY TIME I SEE HIM, IT'S A REVIVAL.

WHAT'S THE SECRET OF HIS SUCCESSFUL CHRISTIAN LIFE?

THIS MAN READS OVER 20 CHAPTERS OF THE BIBLE DAILY, HOLDS DOWN TWO JOBS, PLUS HIS TEACHING MINISTRY.

AM I ASKING YOU TO READ 20 CHAPTERS A DAY? — OF COURSE NOT.

— YOU'RE ONLY GOING TO READ 10 !

LIST OF REASONS WHY YOU CAN'T DO IT.

- I DON'T HAVE THE TIME!
- I'M TOO TIRED!
- I CAN'T FIT IT INTO MY SCHEDULE!
- EVERY TIME I READ IT I GET SLEEPY!
- I DON'T GET ANYTHING OUT OF IT!
- I HATE THE THEES AND THOUS!
- MY WIFE SAYS I LOOK LIKE A FANATIC WHEN I READ IT!

- I DON'T UNDERSTAND THE BIBLE!
- IT'S OFFENSIVE TO MY RELATIVES.
- PEOPLE SAY I'LL LOSE MY MARBLES, IF I READ THAT BOOK!
- BECAUSE IT WORKS ON MY CONSCIENCE!
- I FIND IT BORING!
- I'M ASHAMED OF THE BIBLE!
- I MIGHT GET THE WRONG INTER-PRETATION!

15

OK, OK--- IF I GET ALL THE WAY THROUGH THE BIBLE, *CAN I QUIT?*

ABSOLUTELY NOT!

Do you stop breathing? This is the only way you're going to grow! So you might as well make up your mind that this is now part of your life.

In a very short time, it'll become the most important part of your life.

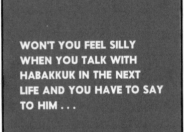

WON'T YOU FEEL SILLY WHEN YOU TALK WITH HABAKKUK IN THE NEXT LIFE AND YOU HAVE TO SAY TO HIM . . .

UH, NO, I DIDN'T READ YOUR BOOK! I DIDN'T EVEN KNOW IT WAS IN THE BIBLE! (GULP)

NOW LET'S GET DOWN TO BUSINESS . . . YOU ARE GOING TO READ TEN CHAPTERS A DAY! BY THE END OF FOUR MONTHS, YOU WILL COVER MORE CHAPTERS THAN THERE ARE IN THE ENTIRE BIBLE (1189).

Here's your tool kit!

- **Colored pencils**
- **A small note book**
- **Bible**

Howbeit when he, the Spirit of truth, is come, he will guide you into all truth: for he shall not speak of himself; but whatsoever he shall hear, that shall he speak: and he will show you things to come.
John 16:13

HEAVENLY FATHER, MAY YOUR BLESSED SPIRIT TEACH AND GUIDE ME IN YOUR TRUTH AS I READ FROM YOUR WORD. IN JESUS' NAME, AMEN.

ALWAYS PRAY BEFORE READING THE WORD.

AS YOU READ CAREFULLY THROUGH EACH CHAPTER, MARK VERSES YOU LIKE WITH A COLORED PENCIL. IF IT IS AN EXCEPTIONAL VERSE, MAKE A MARK IN THE MARGIN NEXT TO IT.

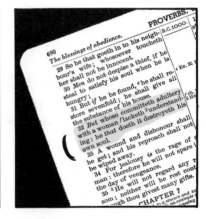

As you go through this program— you will occasionally come across a jewel that's been hiding in a chapter that you have read many times before — The Holy Spirit seems to take the scales from off your eyes and you are delighted.

Put this down in your little note book or you'll soon forget it.

Remember, you are reading God's word.

You may try speed reading and boast about your ability—but your retention rate will be zero!

If you're not getting food, you're reading too fast.

10 CHAPTERS DAILY:
ONE CHAPTER FROM EACH OF THE FOLLOWING 10 LISTS . . .
(START EACH LIST OVER UPON COMPLETION OF THAT LIST.)

LIST **1**	LIST **2**	LIST **3**	LIST **4**
IN 117 DAYS THIS SET WILL BE REPEATED.	IN 187 DAYS THIS SET WILL BE REPEATED.	IN 78 DAYS THIS SET WILL BE REPEATED.	IN 65 DAYS THIS SET WILL BE REPEATED.
MATTHEW	GENESIS	ROMANS	I & II THESS.
MARK	EXODUS	I COR.	I & II TIM.
LUKE	LEVITICUS	II COR.	TITUS
JOHN	NUMBERS	GALATIANS	PHILEMON
ACTS	DEUTERONOMY	EPH.	JAMES
		PHIL.	I & II PETER
		COL.	I, II & III JOHN
		HEBREWS	JUDE.
			REV.

LIST **5**	LIST **6**	LIST **8**	LIST **9**	**9** CONT.
IN 62 DAYS THIS SET WILL BE REPEATED.	IN 150 DAYS THIS SET WILL BE REPEATED.	IN 249 DAYS THIS SET WILL BE REPEATED.	IN 250 DAYS THIS SET WILL BE REPEATED.	NAHUM HAB. ZEPH. HAGG. ZECH. MAL.
JOB ECC. S. SOL	PSALMS	JOSHUA JUDGES RUTH I & II SAM. I & II KINGS I & II CHRON. EZRA NEM. ESTHER	ISA. JER. LAM. EZEKIEL DAN. HOS. JOEL AMOS OBADIAH JONAH MICAH	

For LIST 6, below PSALMS:

LIST **7**
IN 31 DAYS THIS SET WILL BE REPEATED.
PROVERBS

For column 5, below the 9 CONT.:

LIST **10**
ALTERNATELY READ SINGLE CHAPTER DAILY:
HEB. 11 I COR. 13

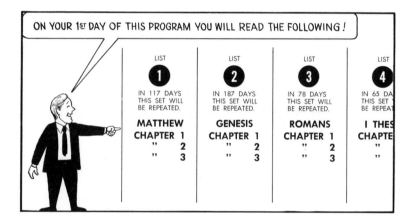

ON YOUR 1ST DAY OF THIS PROGRAM YOU WILL READ THE FOLLOWING !

LIST **1**	LIST **2**	LIST **3**	LIST **4**
IN 117 DAYS THIS SET WILL BE REPEATED.	IN 187 DAYS THIS SET WILL BE REPEATED.	IN 78 DAYS THIS SET WILL BE REPEATED.	IN 65 DA THIS SET BE REPEAT
MATTHEW CHAPTER 1 " 2 " 3	GENESIS CHAPTER 1 " 2 " 3	ROMANS CHAPTER 1 " 2 " 3	I THES CHAPTE "

1	**2**	**3**	**4**	**5**	**6**	**7**	**8**
MATTHEW CHAPTER 2 " 3	GENESIS CHAPTER 2 " 3	ROMANS CHAPTER 2 " 3	I THESS. CHAPTER 2 " 3	JOB CHAPTER 2 " 3	PSALMS CHAPTER 2 " 3	PROVERBS CHAPTER 2 " 3	JOSHUA CHAPTER "

ON THE 2nd DAY, YOU MOVE TO THE 2nd CHAPTER OF EACH GROUP AS INDICATED. ON THE 3rd DAY THE 3rd CHAPTER, ETC.

USE YOUR OWN COLOR CODE TO TRACE YOUR PREVIOUS DAY'S READING. SOON YOUR BIBLE WILL LOOK LIKE A RAINBOW.

1. WHO WAS THE FATHER OF METHUSE-LAH?

2. WHO WERE THE ONLY TWO MEN TO SURVIVE THE FORTY YEARS IN THE WILDERNESS?

3. WHO WAS THE APOSTLE TO THE GENTILES?

4. WHAT IS THE BEGINNING OF WISDOM?

5. DOES ANYONE KNOW THE DAY OR THE HOUR WHEN CHRIST WILL COME?

IN FOUR MONTHS FROM NOW YOU SHOULD BE ABLE TO ANSWER THESE QUESTIONS.

CHAPTER 3

PRAYER

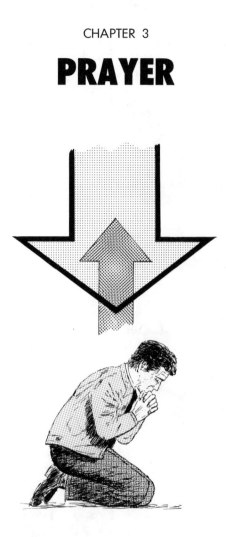

AND IN THE MORNING, RISING UP A GREAT WHILE BEFORE DAY, HE (JESUS) WENT OUT, AND DEPARTED INTO A SOLITARY PLACE, AND THERE PRAYED.

Mark 1:35

Elijah prayed down fire from heaven.
I Kings 18:38

His prayers held back rain for three years — because of Israel's wickedness.
James 5:17

Elijah prayed for rains to come — and the land was refreshed.
James 5:18

The effectual fervent prayer of a righteous man availeth much.
James 5:16

Because Daniel dared to pray — he was put into a den of lions.

God heard his prayers and saved him.

DANIEL SERVED UNDER THESE THREE MEN.

NEBUCHADNEZZAR	BELSHAZZAR	DARIUS
Daniel was Governor over the whole province of Babylon.	Daniel became the third ruler of his kingdom.	Daniel became one of his three presidents.

With all this responsibility, Daniel took time to pray 3 times daily — do you?

22

We now move into the
New Testament and see
the Lord Jesus Christ
pray to His Father
in Heaven.

He would rise up a great
while before day to com-
mune in prayer (Jesus is the
master of prayer)

Mark 1:35

LORD, TEACH
US TO PRAY!

AFTER THIS MANNER THEREFORE PRAY YE:
OUR FATHER WHICH ART IN HEAVEN, HALLOWED BE
THY NAME. THY KINGDOM COME. THY WILL
BE DONE IN EARTH, AS IT IS IN HEAVEN.
GIVE US THIS DAY OUR DAILY BREAD. AND FORGIVE
US OUR DEBTS, AS WE FORGIVE OUR DEBTORS. AND
LEAD US NOT INTO TEMPTATION, BUT DELIVER US
FROM EVIL: FOR THINE IS THE KINGDOM, AND THE
POWER, AND THE GLORY, FOREVER, AMEN.
(MATT. 6, 9-13)

THE LORD GAVE US AN EXAMPLE OF HOW TO PRAY — BUT TO PRAY THIS PRAYER CONSTANTLY IS
VAIN REPETITION.   Matthew 6:7

THIS IS THE PATTERN HE TAUGHT US!

1. YOU ARE TO EXALT THE FATHER.

2. THY KINGDOM COME — REFERS
TO HIS 2ND COMING TO SET
UP HIS MILLENNIAL REIGN.

3. ASK FOR YOUR NECESSITIES
DAILY.

4. WE ASK FOR FORGIVENESS.
WE MUST FORGIVE OTHERS.
Eph. 4:32

5. PRAY FOR PROTECTION FROM
THE DEVIL, AND NOT BE OVER-
COME BY TEMPTATION.
I Corinthians 10:13

6. WE ARE TO GIVE TO THE LORD
—GLORY, POWER AND HONOR.

7. PRAISE HIM AND MAKE YOUR
REQUEST KNOWN.

8. YOU END YOUR PRAYER IN
THE NAME OF THE LORD JESUS
CHRIST.   John 14:13-14

The first public teaching on prayer was given by Jesus in the sermon on the mount.

BUT THOU, WHEN THOU PRAYEST, ENTER INTO THY CLOSET, AND WHEN THOU HAST SHUT THY DOOR, PRAY TO THY FATHER WHICH IS IN SECRET; AND THY FATHER WHICH SEETH IN SECRET SHALL REWARD THEE OPENLY. MATT. 6:6

You must daily have a time of prayer alone with the Father...

because your heavenly Father is waiting to talk to you.

Even though your heart is cold and prayerless — go into the presence of your loving Father.

Do not think of how little you have to bring God, but how much He wants to give you. (Remember — He loves you!)

"YOUR FATHER KNOWETH WHAT THINGS YE HAVE NEED OF, BEFORE YE ASK HIM." MATT. 6:8

THE FASCINATING *STORY OF GEORGE MULLER ILLUSTRATES THIS POINT.

*See: THE DIARY OF GEORGE MÜLLER, GREAT MAN OF PRAYER, compiled by A. J. Rendle Short, Zondervan, 1972.

TAKE 3 SACKS OF FLOUR TO GEORGE MÜLLER

George Müller prays—

FATHER, I NEED 3 SACKS OF FLOUR!

LEDGER

REQUEST
NEED 3 SACKS OF FLOUR.

ANSWER

Knock . . . Knock

LEDGER

REQUEST
NEED 3 SACKS OF FLOUR.

ANSWER
LATE THAT SAME NIGHT

On the day of Pentecost—The Holy Spirit came to dwell in the believers.
Acts 2:2-3

When a person receives Jesus Christ as his personal Savior—he is born again, his sins are washed away—and his body becomes the temple of the Holy Spirit.
1 Cor. 6:19   2 Tim. 1:14

Almost immediately the enemy attacks the new Christian's prayer life.

OBSCENITY & PROFANITY

HOW COULD I THINK OF SUCH THINGS, WHEN I'M IN PRAYER?

WHENEVER THIS OCCURS, PLEAD THE BLOOD OF JESUS AND DEMAND SATAN TO LEAVE IN JESUS' NAME.

Z Z Z Z Z

In a little while he becomes too busy to pray.

If he goes to prayer meetings, he becomes bored listening to long prayers—sometimes he falls asleep—anyway, why should God even listen to his prayers?

If he reads about the great men of prayer like David Brainerd . . .

The new Christian will feel inadequate—but the secret was, David Brainerd prayed in Spirit and Truth.

THE APOSTLE JOHN WRITES TO HIS "LITTLE CHILDREN" (CHRISTIAN BELIEVERS) — "If we say that we have no sin, we deceive ourselves, and the truth is not in us." I John 1:8

"... Christ in you, the hope of glory."

SELF THE FLESH

"The heart is deceitful above all things, and desperately wicked: who can know it?" Jeremiah 17:9

"For the flesh lusteth against the Spirit, and the Spirit against the flesh: and these are contrary the one to the other: so that ye cannot do the things that ye would." Galatians 5:17

MENTALLY ASK THE LORD TO PUT YOU INTO THE GRAVE — TO ALLOW CHRIST FULL REIGN.

"Likewise reckon ye also yourselves to be dead indeed unto sin, but alive unto God through Jesus Christ our Lord." Romans 6:11

THE HOLY SPIRIT

"But ye, beloved, building up yourselves on your most holy faith, praying in the Holy Ghost." Jude 1:20

WHEN YOU PRAY, THE HOLY SPIRIT HELPS YOU.

READ ROMANS 8:26-27

A PRAYER FROM THE LORD:

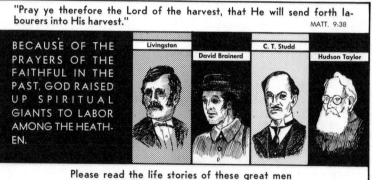

"Pray ye therefore the Lord of the harvest, that He will send forth labourers into His harvest." MATT. 9:38

BECAUSE OF THE PRAYERS OF THE FAITHFUL IN THE PAST, GOD RAISED UP SPIRITUAL GIANTS TO LABOR AMONG THE HEATHEN.

Livingston

David Brainerd

C. T. Studd

Hudson Taylor

Please read the life stories of these great men
You will see the power of prayer.

In a church meeting last month, a missionary leader wept. He begged us to pray to the Lord of harvest to send laborers.

IN INDIA, OVER 50,000 VILLAGES HAVE NEVER HEARD THE NAME OF JESUS!

He said caravans leave Nepal for China and Tibet, that could be carrying Bibles and gospel tracts.

CHINA
NEPAL
INDIA

But they go away empt, because no one is there!

BELOVED, PRAY FOR THE LOST! PRAY — PRAY — PRAY

TRUE STORY

YOU HAVE MY WORD, I'LL PAY YOU BACK

YOU SAVED MY NECK!

A FRIEND OF MINE (A CHRISTIAN) LOANED $3,000 TO A MAN IN SERIOUS TROUBLE.

6 MONTHS LATER

KISS YOUR MONEY GOODBYE *BABY* — BECAUSE I'LL *NEVER* PAY YOU BACK!

3 WEEKS LATER

YAAAAAAA

That man and his girl friend plunged to a Christless grave.

BUT WHOSO SHALL OFFEND ONE OF THESE LITTLE ONES WHICH BELIEVE IN ME, IT WERE BETTER FOR HIM THAT A MILLSTONE WERE HANGED ABOUT HIS NECK, AND THAT HE WERE DROWNED IN THE DEPTH OF THE SEA.

MATT. 18:6

JESUS SAID:
PRAY FOR THOSE WHO DESPITEFULLY USE YOU. — IT IS OUR SOLEMN RESPONSIBILITY.

MY FRIEND FORGOT TO PRAY FOR THAT MAN TO PROTECT HIM FROM GOD'S JUDGMENT.

27

28

CHAPTER 4

LOVE

"BUT GOD COMMENDETH HIS LOVE TO-
WARD US, IN THAT, WHILE WE WERE
YET SINNERS, CHRIST DIED FOR US."

Romans 5:8

30

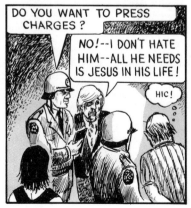

31

I CORINTHIANS — CHAPTER 13

1. "Though I speak with the tongues of men and of angels, and have not *charity, I am become as sounding brass, or a tinkling cymbal.

2. 'And though I have the gift of prophecy, and understand all mysteries, and all knowledge; and though I have all faith, so that I could remove mountains, and have not *charity, I am nothing.

3. 'And though I bestow all my goods to feed the poor, and though I give my body to be burned, and have not *charity, it profiteth me nothing.

4. *Charity suffereth long, and is kind; *charity envieth not; *charity vaunteth not itself, is not puffed up.

5. 'Doth not behave itself unseemly, seeketh not her own, is not easily provoked, thinketh no evil;

6. 'Rejoiceth not in iniquity, but rejoiceth in the truth;

7. 'Beareth all things, believeth all things, hopeth all things, endureth all things.

8. *Charity never faileth: but whether there be prophecies, they shall fail; whether there be tongues, they shall cease; whether there be knowledge, it shall vanish away.

9. 'For we know in part, and we prophesy in part.

10. 'But when that which is perfect is come, then that which is in part shall be done away.

11. 'When I was a child, I spake as a child, I understood as a child, I thought as a child: but when I became a man, I put away childish things.

12. 'For now we see through a glass, darkly; but then face to face: now I know in part; but then shall I know even as also I am known.

13. 'And now abideth faith, hope, *charity, these three; but the greatest of these is *charity."

*Charity (love in action)

33

CHAPTER 5

THE ENEMY

"FOR WE WRESTLE NOT AGAINST FLESH AND BLOOD, BUT AGAINST PRINCIPAL-ITIES, AGAINST POWERS, AGAINST THE RULERS OF THE DARKNESS OF THIS WORLD, AGAINST SPIRITUAL WICKED-NESS IN HIGH PLACES."   Ephesians 6:12

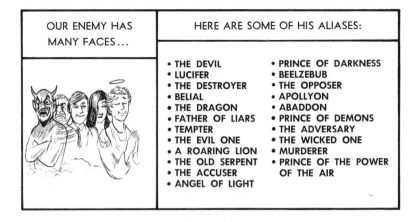

OUR ENEMY HAS MANY FACES...	HERE ARE SOME OF HIS ALIASES:

- THE DEVIL
- LUCIFER
- THE DESTROYER
- BELIAL
- THE DRAGON
- FATHER OF LIARS
- TEMPTER
- THE EVIL ONE
- A ROARING LION
- THE OLD SERPENT
- THE ACCUSER
- ANGEL OF LIGHT

- PRINCE OF DARKNESS
- BEELZEBUB
- THE OPPOSER
- APOLLYON
- ABADDON
- PRINCE OF DEMONS
- THE ADVERSARY
- THE WICKED ONE
- MURDERER
- PRINCE OF THE POWER OF THE AIR

THIS IS THE DEVIL AS THE WORLD SEES HIM.

TRADITION SHOWS HIM WITH A TAIL AND HORNS... ACTUALLY SATAN ORIGINALLY WAS THE MOST BEAUTIFUL CREATURE EVER MADE.　Ezekiel 28:12, 17

LUCIFER'S POSITION WAS ONE OF THE HIGHEST IN HEAVEN... HE GUARDED THE THRONE OF GOD. HIS BEAUTY WAS SO GREAT THAT HE HAD BUILT-IN PIPES FOR MUSIC ... LUCIFER HAD IT MADE.　Ezekiel 28:13-14

SATAN'S MIGHTY DOWNFALL WAS PRIDE.

I WILL ASCEND INTO HEAVEN, I WILL EXHALT MY THRONE ABOVE THE STARS OF GOD: I WILL SIT ALSO UPON THE MOUNT OF THE CONGREGATION IN THE SIDES OF THE NORTH. I WILL ASCEND ABOVE THE HEIGHTS OF THE CLOUDS. I *WILL* BE LIKE THE MOST HIGH!

Isaiah 14:12-14

REBELLION STARTED IN HEAVEN
Isaiah 14:12

A MULTITUDE OF ANGELS JOINED HIM AND THEY DEPARTED FROM GOD'S HEAVEN.

2 Peter 2:4　　Jude 1:6

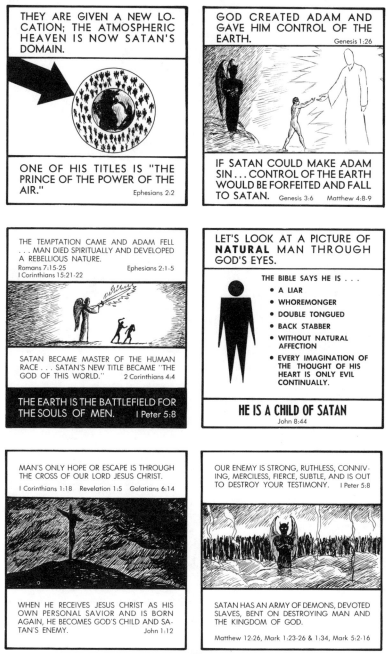

THEY ARE GIVEN A NEW LOCATION; THE ATMOSPHERIC HEAVEN IS NOW SATAN'S DOMAIN.

ONE OF HIS TITLES IS "THE PRINCE OF THE POWER OF THE AIR." Ephesians 2:2

GOD CREATED ADAM AND GAVE HIM CONTROL OF THE EARTH. Genesis 1:26

IF SATAN COULD MAKE ADAM SIN ... CONTROL OF THE EARTH WOULD BE FORFEITED AND FALL TO SATAN. Genesis 3:6 Matthew 4:8-9

THE TEMPTATION CAME AND ADAM FELL ... MAN DIED SPIRITUALLY AND DEVELOPED A REBELLIOUS NATURE.
Romans 7:15-25 Ephesians 2:1-5
I Corinthians 15:21-22

SATAN BECAME MASTER OF THE HUMAN RACE ... SATAN'S NEW TITLE BECAME "THE GOD OF THIS WORLD." 2 Corinthians 4:4

THE EARTH IS THE BATTLEFIELD FOR THE SOULS OF MEN. I Peter 5:8

LET'S LOOK AT A PICTURE OF **NATURAL** MAN THROUGH GOD'S EYES.

THE BIBLE SAYS HE IS . . .
- A LIAR
- WHOREMONGER
- DOUBLE TONGUED
- BACK STABBER
- WITHOUT NATURAL AFFECTION
- EVERY IMAGINATION OF THE THOUGHT OF HIS HEART IS ONLY EVIL CONTINUALLY.

HE IS A CHILD OF SATAN
John 8:44

MAN'S ONLY HOPE OR ESCAPE IS THROUGH THE CROSS OF OUR LORD JESUS CHRIST.
I Corinthians 1:18 Revelation 1:5 Galatians 6:14

WHEN HE RECEIVES JESUS CHRIST AS HIS OWN PERSONAL SAVIOR AND IS BORN AGAIN, HE BECOMES GOD'S CHILD AND SATAN'S ENEMY. John 1:12

OUR ENEMY IS STRONG, RUTHLESS, CONNIVING, MERCILESS, FIERCE, SUBTLE, AND IS OUT TO DESTROY YOUR TESTIMONY. I Peter 5:8

SATAN HAS AN ARMY OF DEMONS, DEVOTED SLAVES, BENT ON DESTROYING MAN AND THE KINGDOM OF GOD.

Matthew 12:26, Mark 1:23-26 & 1:34, Mark 5:2-16

SATAN'S POWER STRUCTURE

THESE ARE 'PRINCES' IN SATAN'S KINGDOM WHO HAVE SECTIONS OR PROVINCES UNDER THEIR CONTROL.

Daniel 10:13

PRINCIPALITIES — THIS REFERS TO POLITICAL REALMS IN WHICH EVIL SPIRITS WORK TO INFLUENCE EARTHLY RULERS, KINGS, PRESIDENTS, PARLIAMENTS, LEGISLATURES, JUDGES, CIVIL OFFICERS, VOTERS, PARTY POLITICS, OFFICE HOLDERS, AND THE ENTIRE RANGE OF MEN AND THINGS CONNECTED WITH THE GOVERNMENT.

WHEN THE LIGHT OF THE GOSPEL GROWS DIM . . . THE GOVERNMENT BECOMES EVIL.

A LARGE SECTION OF SATAN'S FORCES ARE EVIL SPIRITS OF GREAT STRENGTH AND FORCE. THEIR PARTICULAR METHOD OF OPERATION IS TO ATTACK THE PERSONAL FEELINGS AND THOUGHT LIFE OF CHRISTIANS.

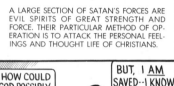

HOW COULD GOD POSSIBLY SAVE SOMEONE AS BAD AS YOU?

BUT, I AM SAVED--I KNOW IT!--I THINK! ---I HOPE! --(GULP)--- OR AM I ???

By grace are ye saved through faith; and that not of yourselves: it is the gift of God: not of works, lest any man should boast.
Ephesians 2:8-9

UNBELIEVERS ARE ALSO ATTACKED IN THIS WAY. THE TERRIBLE CRIMES WE READ ABOUT IN NEWSPAPERS ARE WITHOUT A DOUBT, IN SOME WAY OR OTHER, INSPIRED BY THESE EVIL POWERS. THE METHOD THEY USE WILL DEPEND UPON THE INDIVIDUAL.

SATAN ATTACKS THE WEAK AND DISOBEDIENT CHRISTIAN

- DABBLING IN THE OCCULT
- INTO ASTROLOGY
- NEGLECT IN READING OF THE WORD
- LOVING THE WORLD
- TAKING ONE'S EYES OFF THE LORD
- LUSTING
- DISOBEDIENCE
- PRIDE

HOW CAN A CHRISTIAN GET RID OF THIS PROBLEM?

1. Recognize his need
2. Repent
3. Rebuke it in the name of Jesus
4. Resist the devil and he'll flee from us.
   James 4:7

"Put on the whole armour of God, that ye may be able to stand against the wiles of the devil."
Ephesians 6:11

WHEN A CHRISTIAN IS **DEAD** TO **SELF** AND **ALIVE** TO **GOD** . . .

SATAN WILL FLEE FROM CHRISTIANS WHO ARE . . .

1. **SATURATED WITH THE WORD OF GOD**

2. **WHO ARE FULL OF THE HOLY SPIRIT**

SATAN DOES NOT ATTACK A CHRISTIAN WITHOUT PERMISSION.

1. **NEVER OVERESTIMATE SATAN.**

2. **NEVER UNDERESTIMATE HIM.**

WHEN A CHRISTIAN IS HIT BY SATAN . . .

A. IF HE IS WALKING IN THE LORD, IT IS ALWAYS FOR GOD'S GLORY AND THE CHRISTIAN'S OWN GOOD.

B. IF HE IS **NOT** IN THE LORD, WHEN AFFLICTIONS COME, AND HE COMPLAINS, MURMURS AND REBELS AGAINST GOD AND LOSES HIS TESTIMONY, EVERYONE HOLDS HIM IN CONTEMPT. Matthew 7: 24–27

IN THE OLD TESTAMENT, IN THE BOOK OF JOB . . . GOD PULLS BACK THE CURTAIN AND REVEALS WHAT TOOK PLACE BEHIND THE SCENES.

WHAT DO YOU THINK OF JOB?– THERE IS NONE LIKE HIM ON THE EARTH !

LET *ME* ATTACK HIM-- AND SEE HOW FAITHFUL HE IS !

PERMISSION GRANTED !

NOTICE: JOB WAS INNOCENT AND TOTALLY OBLIVIOUS OF THIS ACTION

JOB WAS SMITTEN WITH BOILS FROM HEAD TO TOE.

CURSE GOD AND DIE !*

THOUGH HE SLAY ME, YET WILL I TRUST IN HIM !**

Job's wife

*Job 2:9   **Job 13:15

SATAN ATTACKED JOB THROUGH HIS WIFE AND FRIENDS . . . THEY JUDGED HIM, NOT IN LOVE, BUT CRITICALLY TO HURT HIM.

AT THE END OF THIS ORDEAL, JOB WAS **GREATLY** BLESSED.

THE DEVIL'S ATTACKS COME IN MANY WAYS
... HERE ARE A FEW ...

1. HE TRIES TO KILL THE CHRISTIAN WITH CRAZY IMPULSES.

2. HE TRIES TO DESTROY THE CHRISTIAN'S TESTIMONY.

3. HE TRIES TO MAKE CHRISTIANS DOUBT THEY ARE REALLY SAVED.

4. HE BRINGS SUBTLE PERSECUTION THROUGH FRIENDS AND RELATIVES.

5. ONE OF HIS GEMS IS DISCOURAGEMENT.

THE INSTANT WE SIN ... WE MUST CONFESS IT TO THE LORD JESUS ...

HE ALREADY KNOWS ABOUT IT, BUT THERE IS AN ACTION TAKING PLACE IN HEAVEN THAT MOST CHRISTIANS ARE TOTALLY UNAWARE OF...HERE IS HOW SATAN APPEARS AS THE ACCUSER OF THE BRETHREN.

LOOK HOW HE OPERATES ON A CHRISTIAN

A GREAT NUMBER OF THEOLOGICAL GRADUATES DO NOT BELIEVE IN A PERSONAL DEVIL

SATAN'S GREATEST ACHIEVEMENT ... IS THAT NO ONE BELIEVES HE EXISTS.

Revelation 12:9 & 20:3

40

ONE OF SATAN'S GREATEST WEAPONS IS RELIGION . . . HERE ARE ONLY A FEW OF HIS RELIGIONS AND GIMMICKS:

• SCIENTOLOGY	• MAOISM	• HARI KRISHNA	• E.S.P.
• BAHA'I	• JUDAHISM	• JEHOVAH WITNESSES	• OUIJA BOARDS
• THEOSOPHY	• CHURCH OF SATAN	• SPIRITISM	• TAROT CARDS
• BUDDHISM	• UNITY	• GAY CHURCH	• PALMISTRY
• HINDUISM	• SCIENCE OF MIND	• ORIENTAL MYSTICISM	• BLACK MAGIC
• TAOISM	• CHRISTIAN SCIENCE	• ROSICRUCIANS	• SATANISM
• MUHAMMADANISM	• METAPHYSICS	• REINCARNATION	• MORMONISM
• CONFUCIANISM	• VOODOO	• STUDY OF ASTROLOGY	• MASONIC ORDERS
• T. M.	• ROMAN CATHOLIC INSTITUTION (SEE "ALBERTO," CRUSADER VOL. 12)		

THEY ALL SIDESTEP THE FACT THAT JESUS CHRIST IS GOD ALMIGHTY ACCORDING TO THE AUTHORIZED BIBLE.

HERE IS ANOTHER SNEAKY TRAP

THE BIBLE THE WORD OF GOD?---*RIDICULOUS!*

SATAN HAS LIBERAL PASTORS SCATTERED THROUGHOUT THE PROTESTANT CHURCHES.

THESE ARE THE 20th CENTURY SADDUCEES

MANY DENY OR PERVERT THE FOLLOWING . . .

1 THE VIRGIN BIRTH
2 THE DEITY OF CHRIST (CHRIST AS CREATOR)
3 THE BLOOD ATONEMENT
4 DEATH, BURIAL AND RESURRECTION
5 2nd COMING OF CHRIST
6 THE BIBLE IS THE INSPIRED WORD OF GOD
7 EVERLASTING PUNISHMENT IN THE LAKE OF FIRE FOR THE UNSAVED.

IF THE PASTOR DENIES ANY OF THE ABOVE.... THEN GET OUT AND FIND A BIBLE PREACHING CHURCH.

DEMON POSSESSION IS MORE PREVALENT TODAY THAN DURING THE TIME OF JESUS.

IN SOME HOSPITALS, PHYSICIANS ARE FACING YOUNG PEOPLE WHO HAVE BEEN IN THE DRUG CULTURE AND INTO THE OCCULT . . . IN CERTAIN CASES MEDICAL TREATMENT IS USELESS . . . THE PHYSICIANS ARE FACING THE UNKNOWN.

I CAN'T UNDERSTAND IT-- *NOTHING* SEEMS TO WORK!

DR. EDWARD ATKINS , M.D. FACED PATIENTS WHO WOULDN'T RESPOND TO MEDICAL TREATMENT, OR PRAYER . . . THIS DOCTOR ACTUALLY ENCOUNTERED THE POWERS OF DARKNESS, AND IN THE NAME OF JESUS, EXPELLED THEM.

Guideposts, August '72

THE END IS IN SIGHT FOR SATAN

THE ENEMY OF OUR SOULS IS **NOT** DIVINE. SATAN IS ONLY A CREATED BEING. HE IS A FALLEN ANGEL WHOSE ULTIMATE END WILL BE THE LAKE OF FIRE. HE DOUBLE-CROSSES ALL WHO FOLLOW HIM. HE SETS UP WARS AND PUTS MULTITUDES INTO HELL. HE PROMISES POWER AND WEALTH TO THOSE WHO TRUST IN HIM. THEN HE PULLS THE RUG OUT FROM UNDER THEM.

HE IS A DESTROYER AND A CRUEL MASTER. HIS FOLLOWERS TURN TO DRUGS, LIQUOR, ETC., AND END UP WITH DISEASE, MISERY, AND EVENTUALLY GO TO CHRISTLESS GRAVES.
THE BIBLE TELLS US THAT SATAN WILL BE CONQUERED BY THE LORD JESUS AT HIS SECOND COMING.

JESUS TAKES OVER WORLD GOVERNMENT IN JERUSALEM . . .

SATAN IS BOUND FOR 1000 YEARS. AT THE END OF THE MILLENIUM, SATAN IS LOOSED FOR A LITTLE SEASON TO DECEIVE THE NATIONS . . . **THEN HE IS ALSO CAST INTO THE LAKE OF FIRE.

**Revelation 20:10

THIS IS THE END OF SATAN!

ALL THOSE WHO DIED IN THEIR SINS WILL SPEND ETERNITY WITH HIM. Revelation 20:15, 21:8

JESUS IS LORD !!!

"They that see thee shall narrowly look upon thee, and consider thee, saying, Is this the man that made the earth to tremble, that did shake kingdoms;" Isaiah 14:16

BUT IF YOU'RE A BORN AGAIN BELIEVER IN CHRIST . . . REJOICE! YOU WILL REIGN WITH THE LORD JESUS IN GLORY. Revelation 5:10

CHAPTER 6

PITFALLS

"But put ye on the Lord Jesus Christ, and make not provision for the flesh, to fulfill the lusts thereof." Romans 13:14

MANY VIBRANT CHRISTIANS HAVE BEEN SET ASIDE BECAUSE THEIR TESTIMONIES WERE RUINED.

I Corinthians 9:27

. . . AND IT CAN BE RUINED BY SUCH A LITTLE ACT.

WHY THAT ⓒ!!!⚡⚡ THIEF!

"Providing for honest things not only in the sight of the Lord, but also in the sight of men."
II Corinthians 8:21

I'LL GET THAT PHONEY ON THE NEXT LAYOFF! —CHRISTIAN MY FOOT! — IT'LL BE A FROSTY FRIDAY IN *H----*! BEFORE I *EVER* BECOME ONE!

SMITH BLEW HIS TESTIMONY . . . HE BECAME A CASTAWAY.
I Corinthians 9:27

SOME CHRISTIAN WORKERS HAVE BEEN LAID ASIDE BECAUSE THEY FAILED TO HAVE A PARTNER ACCOMPANY THEM ON A VISIT TO A PERSON OF THE OPPOSITE SEX. SATAN TAKES ADVANTAGE OF THIS TYPE OF SITUATION AND THEY FALL INTO SIN.

YOU SAY IT CAN'T HAPPEN TO YOU?

KING DAVID WAS 50 YEARS OLD WHEN HE SAW BATHSHEBA.
Read II Samuel, Chapter 11

TODAY SEX IS DISPLAYED EVERYWHERE

SOME GOOD SOURCES OF STRENGTH TO HELP YOU RESIST THIS SIN CAN BE FOUND BY READING THE FOLLOWING . . . .

Genesis, Chapter 39
Proverbs, Chapters 6 & 7
I Corinthians 6:18
I Corinthians 7:1-3

BE CONSTANTLY ON GUARD . . . YOU CAN RUIN YOUR TESTIMONY AND BECOME USELESS FOR THE LORD.

CHAPTER 7

CALLED OUT

"Wherefore come out from among them, and be ye separate, saith the Lord, and touch not the unclean thing; and I will receive you."

II Corinthians 6:17

AM I AN AMBASSADOR ?

*NOT ONLY AN AMBASSADOR OF CHRIST, BUT YOU ARE *NOW* A CHILD OF GOD, INSTEAD OF THE DEVIL!
YOU'RE A JOINT HEIR WITH CHRIST— AND YOU WILL RULE WITH HIM THROUGHOUT ETERNITY!

©!!✳✳ I HATE PEOPLE LIKE THAT!

OLD HOLIER THAN THOU!

*2 Corinthians 5:20; John 1:12; Romans 8:17; Romans 8:28; II Timothy 2:10; II Timothy 2:12

JESUS SAID, "IF THE WORLD HATE YOU, YE KNOW THAT IT HATED ME BEFORE IT HATED YOU."

John 15:18

I'M GOING TO RULE ???

YOU ARE OF THE *ROYAL PRIESTHOOD, A KING, A PRIEST.**IN FACT, IF GOD GAVE YOU A PICTURE OF YOUR FUTURE WITH HIM NOW, YOUR MIND COULDN'T HANDLE IT.
**I Cor. 2:9

*I Peter 2:5; Revelation 1:6

MAN, THEN I'M REALLY SOMETHING !

"WHEREFORE, LET HIM THAT THINKETH HE STANDETH, TAKE HEED LEST HE FALL."
I COR. 10:12

YOUR ATTITUDE IS FULL OF PRIDE ! *REMEMBER*, YOU ARE <u>NOTHING</u> WITHOUT CHRIST !

HOW SHOULD I ACT? LIKE A KING?

NO, LIKE A SERVANT!--- CHRIST IS OUR EXAMPLE! *HE SINNED NOT, HE NEVER ANSWERED BACK WHEN HE WAS INSULTED----WHEN HE SUFFERED, HE NEVER THREATENED TO GET EVEN....... HE LEFT HIS CASE IN THE HANDS OF GOD, WHO ALWAYS JUDGES FAIRLY!

*I Peter 2:23

BUT, I CAN'T* TURN THE OTHER CHEEK!

YOU CAN, IF YOU ARE **DEAD TO YOURSELF AND ALIVE TO CHRIST. ONLY THEN, THE HOLY SPIRIT TAKES CONTROL AND THEN YOU HAVE THE POWER† TO SUFFER FOR HIS SAKE!

*Luke 6:29

**Romans 6:11-12
†Philippians 1:29

BUT THEY WON'T RESPECT ME!

*WHEN THEY SEE CHRIST IN YOU --- THEY WILL SEE YOUR GOOD WORKS AND GLORIFY YOUR FATHER WHICH IS IN HEAVEN!

*Matthew 5:16

*John 17:14   **Joshua 1:8 & Psalm 1:2   †I Peter 2:2   ‡2 Peter 3:18

CHAPTER 8

WARN THEM

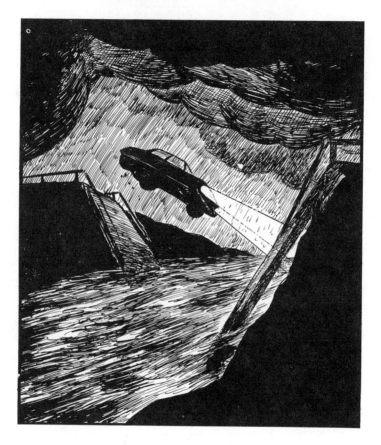

"When I say unto the wicked, Thou shalt surely die; and thou givest him not warning, nor speakest to warn the wicked from his wicked way, to save his life; the same wicked man shall die in his iniquity; but his blood will I require at thine hand."

Ezekiel 3:18

"Let him know, that he which converteth the sinner from the error of his way, shall save a soul from death, and shall hide a multitude of sins."

James 5:20

THE GREAT COMMISSION THAT JESUS GAVE TO HIS FOLLOWERS IS THIS...

GO YE INTO ALL THE WORLD AND PREACH THE *GOSPEL TO EVERY CREATURE!

*GOOD NEWS . . . CHRIST DIED FOR YOUR SINS.

*Mark 16:15

NOW THAT I'M SAVED, I WANT TO GO TELL OTHERS!

HEY EVERYBODY, I'M SAVED! ARE YOU?

NO!   NO!

WHAT DID I DO WRONG? CAN YOU HELP ME?

YES!

FIRST . . . YOU MUST HAVE A PLAN TO WIN THE BATTLE.

THERE IS LESS CONFUSION IF YOU USE A PLAN IN ONE BOOK OF THE BIBLE.

ONE OF THE BEST PRESENTATIONS OF A GROUP OF SUCH SCRIPTURES . . .

IS CALLED . . .
"THE ROMAN ROAD"

TO BE A SOUL WINNER, YOU SHOULD GET YOURSELF A SMALL NEW TESTAMENT.

THIS IS A BAD APPROACH!

WHEN THEY SEE IT, THEY GET SCARED.

YOU MUST FIRST PREPARE YOUR LITTLE NEW TESTAMENT WITH GUIDE NOTES, FOR YOUR OWN BENEFIT.

TAKE A COLORED PEN OR PENCIL AND TURN TO THE BOOK OF ROMANS . . .

YOUR FIRST VERSE IS ROMANS CHAPTER 3 AND VERSE 10.

NOW THAT YOU'VE MARKED IT LIKE WE HAVE ABOVE, YOU MOVE TO THE NEXT VERSE.

THE NEXT VERSE IS ROMANS CHAPTER 3 AND VERSE 23.

ALWAYS INDICATE IN THE MARGIN THE NEXT VERSE YOU ARE TO READ.

HERE IS THE LIST YOU WILL FOLLOW ON THE ROMAN ROAD . . .

① ROMANS 3:10		⑥ ROMANS 10:13
② ROMANS 3:23		⑦ *REVELATION 3:20
③ ROMANS 5:12		⑧ ROMANS 10:9-10
④ ROMANS 5:8		*This is an excellent, but not required, detour point from the plan.
⑤ ROMANS 6:23		

MARK ALL OF THESE DOWN IN YOUR NEW TESTAMENT — SO YOU WON'T MAKE ANY MISTAKES.

LET'S SEE-- FIRST IT'S ROMANS-UH 16-- NO, IT'S ---UH,12?

WITH THIS TECHNIQUE, YOU DON'T HAVE TO MEMORIZE THE SCRIPTURES . . . (THAT WILL COME IN TIME AS YOU USE THE SYSTEM.)

BEFORE WITNESSING, PRAY, ASKING GOD FOR POWER THROUGH THE HOLY SPIRIT. ASK HIM TO USE YOU TO WIN SOMEONE FOR CHRIST.

NEVER HIT THEM COLD WITH A QUESTION LIKE . . . "HAVE YOU BEEN SAVED?"

WHAT KIND OF WORK DO YOU DO?

I'M A CARPENTER!

TALK ABOUT THE WEATHER OR THEIR JOB FOR A FEW MINUTES.

MAY I ASK YOU A QUESTION?

SURE, GO AHEAD!

"IF YOU WERE TO DIE TONIGHT . . . ARE YOU SURE YOU WOULD GO TO HEAVEN?"

ANY REPLY LESS THAN 100% CERTAINTY, IS A SIGN YOU MUST PRESENT THE ROMAN ROAD.

IF IT WERE POSSIBLE TO KNOW FOR SURE THAT YOU COULD GO TO HEAVEN--WOULD YOU BE INTERESTED?

I'D BE A *NUT* IF I DIDN'T!

IF I COULD SHOW YOU HOW YOU CAN KNOW FROM THE BIBLE, WOULD YOU DO WHAT THE BIBLE SAYS ?

SURE !

PEOPLE AREN'T ALWAYS INTERESTED. SOME GET ANGRY. BE PLEASANT, LEAVE A TRACT, AND GO TALK TO SOMEONE ELSE.

ROMANS 3:10 POINTS OUT THAT I'M *NOT* RIGHTEOUS AND YOU'RE NOT EITHER. ROMANS 3:23 SAYS WE ALL FALL SHORT OF GOD'S STANDARD !

POINT OUT THAT YOU ARE A SINNER FIRST, THEN THAT HE IS ALSO. NEVER PUT THE SINNER BELOW YOU.

THE NEXT POINT REFERS TO ROMANS 5:12

IN THE BEGINNING, GOD AND ADAM'S HEARTS WERE KNIT TOGETHER — THROUGH ADAM'S DISOBEDIENCE THEIR SWEET TOGETHERNESS WAS BROKEN. ADAM DIED BOTH SPIRITUALLY AND PHYSICALLY

WE INHERIT SPIRITUAL AND PHYSICAL DEATH FROM OUR PARENTS, ADAM AND EVE.

NOW, MOVE TO ROMANS 5:8

HUMM !

HERE WE FIND CHRIST DIED ON THE CROSS, HE BECAME OUR SUBSTITUTE BY TAKING OUR PLACE !

ROMANS 6:23 — "THE WAGES OF SIN IS DEATH . . ."

MOST OF US WORK FOR WAGES. OUR PAY FOR BEING A SINNER IS DEATH !

WHY DID ADAM LISTEN TO EVE, AND SIN ?

WE'LL COME BACK TO THAT LATER !

WARNING: NEVER GET OFF THE ROMAN ROAD BY ARGUING DOCTRINE OR OPINION!

". . . BUT THE GIFT OF GOD IS ETERNAL LIFE."

IF SOMEONE GIVES YOU A GIFT AND YOU RECEIVE IT, YOU KNOW YOU HAVE IT --- *RIGHT* ?

RIGHT !

WHY DON'T YOU COME TO CHURCH WITH ME AND MAKE A PUBLIC CONFESSION OF YOUR FAITH?

I WILL, THANK YOU!

YOU HAVE JUST BEEN BORN AGAIN SPIRITUALLY AND YOU NEED TO GROW UP. THE BIBLE IS OUR SPIRITUAL FOOD — YOU MUST READ IT DAILY!

WHEN YOU LEAD SOMEONE TO CHRIST GIVE THEM A COPY OF THIS BOOK PUBLISHED BY CHICK PUBLICATIONS.

THE NEXT STEP
FOR GROWING CHRISTIANS

By J.T.C.

THIS WILL GET THEM GOING IN THE RIGHT DIRECTION.

THE MORE YOU KNOW ABOUT SCRIPTURE — THE EASIER IT IS TO PRESENT THE ROMAN ROAD.

ROMANS 3:10

3:23

YOU'RE NOT TO BE DISCOURAGED WHEN I TELL YOU, THAT YOU'RE *NOT* GOING TO SAVE ANYONE!

HOW COME?

WE'RE TO BE A WITNESS FOR GOD. HE PREPARES THE HEART. *HE* DRAWS THE SINNER AND *HE* DOES THE SAVING!

HERE ARE SOME IMPORTANT RULES.

1. GO NEATLY DRESSED — YOU REPRESENT THE KING OF KINGS.
2. WATCH YOUR BREATH — USE BREATH MINTS.
3. GO WITH A PARTNER IF POSSIBLE.

REMEMBER, THE EYES OF THE WORLD ARE LOOKING FOR CHRIST IN YOU.

THERE ARE TIMES WHEN YOU CANNOT DEAL PERSONALLY WITH SOMEONE ABOUT CHRIST.

BUT THERE IS **SOMETHING** YOU **CAN** DO.

YOU CAN TAKE ADVANTAGE OF OUR HIGHLY SUCCESSFUL TRACT MINISTRY.

WHO, ME?

WHY NOT?

WITH THESE LITTLE BOOKLETS, YOU CAN START YOUR OWN PROGRAM BY YOURSELF.

WE HAVE A FINE SELECTION TO CHOOSE FROM.

DO THEY WORK?

ONE FRIEND TOLD US THAT OVER 500 WERE SAVED IN HIS AREA AS A RESULT OF THESE BOOKLETS.

GOD BLESS YOU AS YOU START ON ONE OF THE MOST EXCITING ADVENTURES OF YOUR LIFE.

OVER 70 TITLES AVAILABLE!

See a complete list of Chick titles on World Wide Web at: http://chick.com

EACH BOOKLET A PROVEN SOUL WINNER!

God dealt with my heart after reading **THIS WAS YOUR LIFE!** and saved my lost soul. Have used Chick tracts ever since! R.J., Lancaster, VA

To say that Chick tracts get read is an understatement. Our church orders and stocks a lot of Chick tracts and I can honestly say that they get read at a rate of six to one over the other tracts. R.B., Hamilton, OH

Thank you so much for your tracts. My son-in-law was recently saved. I used your tracts one by one to share with him! S.R., Flagstaff, AZ

I use your tracts **ONE WAY** and **BIG DADDY** with the children I teach. They help explain the plan of salvation in a way which captures their interest right away. Many have been won to the Lord. L.D., Separta, MI

I have just read **THIS WAS YOUR LIFE!** I was fortunate enough to run across it in a restaurant; it was left on my table by someone. It brought me to tears and I was, for the first time, confronted with my own life and how I led it. I never thought one little booklet could bring about so much of a change. J.H., Richmond, VA

THESE SOUL WINNING BOOKLETS CAN BE OBTAINED AT YOUR LOCAL GOSPEL BOOKSTORE OR FROM CHICK PUBLICATIONS, P.O. BOX 662, CHINO, CA 91708-0662

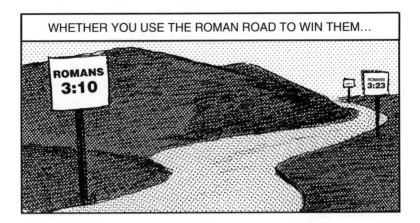

WHETHER YOU USE THE ROMAN ROAD TO WIN THEM...

OR
ILLUSTRATED
GOSPEL
LITERATURE

REMEMBER... IF YOU DON'T TELL THEM, WHO WILL?

IN THE FUTURE, AT THE JUDGMENT SEAT OF CHRIST . . . CHRISTIANS WILL RECEIVE THEIR REWARDS BASED ON THEIR FAITHFULNESS.

GOD HAS GIVEN US GIFTS . . . AND WE ARE STEWARDS OF THESE GIFTS . . . WE ALL HAVE ONE OR MORE OF THEM.

Ephesians 4:7-8

INCORRUPTIBLE CROWNS WILL BE AWARDED.

HERE ARE ONLY A FEW . . .

- PRAYING
- SINGING
- PREACHING
- TEACHING
- SOUL WINNING
- WITNESSING

- SERVING, SUCH AS MOPPING FLOORS UNTO THE LORD.
- LIVING CHRIST BEFORE OTHERS.
- GIVING (TIME OR MONEY).

	THESE ARE OBTAINED BY
CROWN OF GLORY	• PRACTISING SELF-CONTROL
CROWN OF LIFE	• SOUL WINNING
	• OBEDIENCE
CROWN OF RIGHTEOUSNESS	• FAITHFUL MINISTERS FEEDING THEIR FLOCKS
SOUL WINNER'S CROWN	• JOYFULLY ENDURING TRIALS AND TESTING.

WHEN IT IS ALL OVER, WE WILL WORSHIP HIM AND CAST OUR CROWNS AT HIS FEET.
Revelation 4:10

HERE IS ANOTHER VIEW . . . THIS HAS NOTHING TO DO WITH YOUR SALVATION BECAUSE THOSE WHO WERE BORN AGAIN HAVE HAD THEIR SINS WASHED AWAY BY THE BLOOD OF CHRIST.

FOR WE MUST ALL APPEAR BEFORE THE JUDGEMENT SEAT OF CHRIST, SO THAT EACH ONE MAY RECEIVE (HIS REWARD) ACCORDING TO WHAT HE HAS DONE IN THE BODY, WHETHER GOOD OR EVIL (CONSIDERING WHAT HIS MOTIVES AND PURPOSES HAVE BEEN, AND WHAT HE HAS ACHIEVED).
READ 2 CORINTHIANS 5:10

OUR WORKS WILL BE TESTED . . . READ CAREFULLY I CORINTHIANS 3:11-15.

MANY OF US WILL BE IN FOR A BIG SURPRISE.

THINK OFTEN ABOUT THE JUDGMENT SEAT OF CHRIST. WHAT YOU DO NOW DETERMINES THE POSITION YOU'LL HOLD WITH CHRIST THROUGHOUT ALL ETERNITY.

WHAT WILL YOU DO IN HEAVEN?

- YOU WILL JUDGE ANGELS . . . I Cor. 6:3
- YOU WILL REIGN WITH CHRIST ON EARTH AND IN THE HEAVENLIES.
2 Tim. 2:12
- YOU WILL BE WITNESSES AT THE GREAT WHITE THRONE JUDGMENT.
Rev. 20:11-15

- YOU WILL JUDGE THE WORLD.
I Cor. 6:2
- ATTEND THE MARRIAGE SUPPER OF THE LAMB.
Rev. 19:7
IF GOD REVEALED TO US THE GLORIES THAT AWAIT US . . . IT WOULD BLOW OUR MINDS.
2 Corinthians 12:4

"Therefore, my beloved brethren, be ye stedfast, unmoveable, always abounding in the work of the Lord, forasmuch as ye know that your labour is not in vain in the Lord.   I Corinthians 15:58